One-Minute Prayers™

FROM THE *Bible*

Text by Hope Lyda

HARVEST HOUSE PUBLISHERS

EUGENE, OREGON

Cover by Garborg Design Works, Minneapolis, Minnesota

ONE-MINUTE PRAYERS is a series trademark of The Hawkins Children's LLC. Harvest House Publishers, Inc. is the exclusive licensee of the trademark ONE-MINUTE PRAYERS.

ONE-MINUTE PRAYERS™ FROM THE BIBLE
Copyright © 2005 by Harvest House Publishers
Published by Harvest House Publishers
Eugene, Oregon 97402

ISBN 0-7369-1557-5

Printed in the United States of America

05 06 07 08 09 10 11 12   / BP-MS /   10 9 8 7 6 5 4 3

Contents

Prayer

Our Father in heaven,
hallowed be your name,
your kingdom come,
your will be done
on earth as it is in heaven.
Give us this day our daily bread.
Forgive us our debts,
as we also have forgiven our debtors.
And lead us not into temptation,
but deliver us from the evil one,
for yours is the kingdom and the power and the
glory forever. Amen.

MATTHEW 6:9-13

God in heaven and all around me, I thank You for hearing the prayers of Your child. May I pray with a heart of humility that receives Your will and guidance and grace without my own judgments getting in the way. Lord, grant me the sense of hope I need to truly engage in communication with my Creator. Lead me into times of open dialogue with You. Bring me to my knees so that I can be humble enough to open my mind, heart, and spirit to receive Your love and to fully feel Your power and glory. Amen.

Receiving

Ready to Believe

Jesus replied, "I tell you the truth, if you have faith and do not doubt, not only can you do what was done to the fig tree, but also you can say to this mountain, 'Go, throw yourself into the sea,' and it will be done. If you believe, you will receive whatever you ask for in prayer."

MATTHEW 21:21-22

My prayers do not always reflect a faith of true believing, Lord. I find myself asking without faith in the outcome, without fully trusting that You are listening. Fill my heart with faith that leaves no room for doubt. Let my questions be those of a seeker desiring a deeper relationship with You, rather than those of a person who places obstacles between my life and the One who made it.

As I practice the discipline of prayer, may it make me ready to receive all that is good, holy, and of You. May my lips never release words that are not lifted up in faith.

Receive Me

Take words with you and return to the LORD. Say to him: "Forgive all our sins and receive us graciously, that we may offer the fruit of our lips."

HOSEA 14:2

Receive me, Lord. Take my enthusiasm, my questions, my willingness, and shape them into someone who seeks only what is of You and from Your hand. Receive my efforts and clean away the sin that can taint the good things that can come from my life.

Receive my words, hear them within Your sweet grace so that they are pleasing to You. May my expressed thoughts and prayers be my promise of ongoing dialogue. My desire to reach You and to be held in Your hand has become a longing. My heart is full as You receive Your child's simple words, faltering praises, and pleading inquiries.

The Whole Me

Do not reject me or forsake me, O God my Savior.
Though my father and mother forsake me, the LORD
will receive me. Teach me your way, O LORD; lead
me in a straight path because of my oppressors.

PSALM 27:9-11

There are times when people in my life do not understand me. Or maybe they see only a part of me, rather than the whole. This has occurred so many times that I thought it was the only way to be viewed...in pieces. But Lord, You receive me as a whole being. You see the good, the bad, and the desire to do right.

I expect a lot out of people, those close to me and even those I just happen to meet. Help me to understand that even if they let me down or forsake that part of me that they know, this does not define my life. This does not keep me from the path You have laid out before me. I pray to become the whole person You created me to be so that You will receive me with joy.

Accept My Praise

Accept, O Lord, the willing praise of my mouth,
and teach me your laws.

PSALM 119:108

Do You look at the way I live out my faith and consider my praise worthy of Your attention, Lord? Are my prayers of praise acceptable offerings? I do not always know what to say to honor all that You are. Search my heart to discover the depth of my love and gratitude. May what You find be pleasing.

Though it can take me a while to get through my prayers to my praises, Lord, they are willing offerings and reflect the spirit I aspire to have every waking moment.

Humility

One of Many

Praise awaits you, O God, in Zion; to you our vows will be fulfilled. O you who hear prayer, to you all men will come. When we were overwhelmed by sins, you forgave our transgressions.

PSALM 65:1-3

I know I am one of many of Your creations. I know my voice is one of many that rises to be heard in this world…heard by You. My simple sin today is one of many in my lifetime…my journey covered with blemishes that undermine the beauty of the life I could be living. And even though I am one of many who praise You and call You God, You listen to every prayer that leaves my lips.

I am humbled, overwhelmed, and truly thankful for Your presence in my life. When I pray, I am no longer one of many. I am the one You care for and listen to.

Timidity

May my supplication come before you; deliver me
according to your promise. May my lips overflow
with praise, for you teach me your decrees.

PSALM 119:170-71

I can be shy about approaching You. Sometimes I
am a young child who is not certain what to say or how
to find my way through a prayer to get to the heart of
the matter. But when I release my inhibitions and come
to You with a humble and open spirit, my mouth overflows with all that is in me. My gratitude, my concern,
my questions…they all pour forth. I am surprised by
how quickly I become like a pair of open hands, waiting
to receive what You give to fill me.

May my timidity turn to humility so I do not stand
on the sidelines, too nervous to approach You. I long to
run to Your side, bursting with courage, love, and gratitude as I tell You about my day, with no holding back.

The Grace of Knowing

He has showed you, O man, what is good. And what
does the LORD require of you? To act justly and to
love mercy and to walk humbly with your God.

MICAH 6:8

Lord, lately I need a softer heart, a less judgmental mind, a more open spirit. I sense Your leading when I am with other people, yet my very human tendencies stop me from doing what You require of me. Please give me compassionate eyes that see only the need and beauty in people. May my thoughts turn to how You wish for me to interact with someone, rather than how I want to take control of the situation.

Remind me, Lord, that justice and mercy are the cornerstones of my faith. Let me pass along these gifts to other people so that my humility becomes the source of my response to Your children.

Communication

Did I Just Say That?

May the words of my mouth and the meditation of my heart be pleasing in your sight, O LORD, my Rock and my Redeemer.

PSALM 19:14

Did that bit of gossip just come from me? Did I just vent and leave my coworker frustrated? Was it my voice that commented negatively on someone's best efforts? Grant me wisdom and the ability to self-censor, Lord. How often I waste precious time trying to fix something that I ruined by speaking with reckless words. Let the messages that come from me be ones that build up, inspire, and reflect my Redeemer's heart.

May I continue to seek the peace of my faith so that I will not speak unthinkingly from a restless heart, but will speak only from an unwavering desire to please You.

Words for You

My lips will shout for joy when I sing praise to you—I, whom you have redeemed.

PSALM 71:23

As words of encouragement leave my lips, I realize that whether I am talking to myself, a friend, a child, or a coworker, I am also speaking to You, Lord. I have not always taken spiritual responsibility for the words that come from me. I would write them off as appropriate for the circumstance or incited by the situation. But lately, as I consider each word to be spoken for You to hear, I weigh each word. Does it praise my Redeemer? Does it offer someone else a gift in any way? Or is it meant to ease my fear, my insecurity?

Lord, grant me a new vocabulary so that my everyday conversations become praises and shouts for joy.

Listen to Me

Hear my cry, O God; listen to my prayer.

PSALM 61:1

Sometimes I can speak all day and not feel heard. I might as well be invisible or mute. Those days start to take away my sense of meaning and purpose, of connection to the world around me. Today is one of those days. All I ask is to be heard, Lord. Please listen to my prayer and turn Your heart and ear to my whispered thoughts.

To be heard is to have validation. Each time I fall to my knees and talk to You, I understand who I am. I know that I have purpose. You hear what I say between the words. Even my silence shapes my identity in You, Lord. Hear my cry. Listen to my prayer.

Faith

Immediately the boy's father exclaimed, "I do believe; help me overcome my unbelief!"

MARK 9:24

Lord, as I make my way through life with a heart that has faith, I find I still must return to You and ask for Your help to believe. This does not reflect my belief in Your presence or Your truth. It reflects how I feel about myself in this world. I move questions from the tip of my mind to the depths of my soul each day to make room for work, conversation, polite interaction, and the status quo. But eventually they surface. And when they do, I pray for answers. I pray for Your presence. I pray for faith.

I do believe, Lord. Help me overcome my unbelief.

Hope

The Journey to Hope

When you have entered the land the LORD your God is giving you as an inheritance and have taken possession of it and settled in it, take some of the firstfruits of all that you produce from the soil of the land the LORD your God is giving you and put them in a basket. Then go to the place the LORD your God will choose as a dwelling for his Name and say to the priest in office at the time, "I declare today to the LORD your God that I have come to the land the LORD swore to our forefathers to give us."

DEUTERONOMY 26:1-3

You are the God of promises. I receive an inheritance of hope and possibility because You give to Your children an expanse of life to cultivate. I may not own a plot of land, but I do have permission to care for this life, tend to it, and seek Your will for its harvest.

I exist because of the generations of my family before me. My faith and hope exist because of my salvation in You. Today I will take some of the firstfruits from these legacies and enter my future with proof of Your goodness.

Calling Out to You

From the ends of the earth I call to you, I call as my heart grows faint; lead me to the rock that is higher than I. For you have been my refuge, a strong tower against the foe.

PSALM 61:2-3

Even in the most confusing times of my life, I have been able to call out to You with a heart filled with hope. When I can barely keep my eyes open another minute because I am weary, You lead me to a place where I can rest. When I am afraid, You calm my spirit and show me the view ahead that is clear and secure.

For as long as I have known You, I have had a sense of Your love. I know it is okay to be here, in this moment, and not know what will happen tomorrow. Each day You lead me to a place higher than the day before.

Inner Strength

For you have been my hope, O Sovereign LORD, my confidence since my youth. From birth I have relied on you; you brought me forth from my mother's womb. I will ever praise you.

PSALM 71:5-6

Lord, You make me a survivor. It is by Your grace that I have walked through hard times in order to experience joy, peace, or change on the other side. I hold tightly to the peace I have in You. Even in the early days of my youth, when I did not know what to call You, I knew of Your hope. It was built into my spirit, woven into my DNA.

Thank You, Lord. You are the one Force in my life to which I can turn. There are times when I perhaps rely on You too much, but I would rather be this kind of person than one unable to tap into the inner hope of Your Spirit. Praise You, Lord.

All the Livelong Day

Show me your ways, O L ORD, teach me your paths;
guide me in your truth and teach me, for you are
God my Savior, and my hope is in you all day long.

PSALM 25:4-5

By three o'clock in the afternoon, I have very little
to offer anyone. My energy plummets and my enthusiasm wanes. But in my spirit there is still an ember that
burns bright with hope. When my human nature is
ready to nap or give up, I pray that the strength of my
faith and the teachings of Your way will guide me. I do
not want to miss opportunities because I am worn-out
or discouraged.

Inspire in me the hope that rekindles the faith of
other people. Guide me. Teach me. Lead me when I am
struggling to find the right path. Then other people will
see that my belief is not misplaced and that You are not
only my God, but You are my Savior, my strength, and
my eternal hope.

Encouragement

Traveling Together

*May the God who gives endurance and encourage-
ment give you a spirit of unity among yourselves as
you follow Christ Jesus, so that with one heart and
mouth you may glorify the God and Father of our
Lord Jesus Christ.*

ROMANS 15:5-6

Lord, I have figured out that the people I call
friends, and those who rub me the wrong way, and
those I love more than life itself...they are all fellow
travelers. And as we each try to find our footing to take
a step forward, we learn to depend on these other folks.
What better way to inspire strength and perseverance
and unity than to encourage other people on the
journey.

Right now I feel strong and able to give to people
besides myself. I lift up Your name and know Your
strength is behind my words. When my body grows
weary and the weight of life is too much for me, I pray
that another traveler will offer me the spirit of unity and
fellowship with words that come from You, just in time
to inspire me to continue.

Never Ending

*May our Lord Jesus Christ himself and God our
Father, who loved us and by his grace gave us
eternal encouragement and good hope, encourage
your hearts and strengthen you in every good deed
and word.*

2 THESSALONIANS 2:16-17

My ability to be optimistic seems to be limited. I
spark joy for about half a day, determined to be a great
Christian representative to the world, and then I falter.
I stumble. I mumble. Oh, how I must seem so incon-
sistent. God, I want Your encouragement, Your hope,
and Your peace to be evident in my life, even when my
human attempts at optimism fade or the caffeine wears
off. Give me a light from within that encourages other
people.

The idea of eternal, forever, and never-ending
encouragement and hope becomes a foundation on
which to build a life. When I do falter or fall flat on my
face, I pray to draw from this never-ending hope. May
my words and actions be buoyed up once again.

What Keeps Me Going

But you, O LORD, have mercy on me; raise me up,
that I may repay them. I know that you are pleased
with me, for my enemy does not triumph over me.
In my integrity you uphold me and set me in your
presence forever.

PSALM 41:10-12

Knowing that You exist keeps me going. When I doubt all other things around me or face troubles that seem impossible to overcome, Your presence keeps me sane. I pray for Your mercy today, that You will find it right and good to lift me up out of this current circumstance.

I follow Your precepts, Lord. I seek Your heart and wisdom. Please keep me close, in the warmth of Your presence, so that I do not lose sight of what is to come. Encourage me with glimpses of triumph and peace. I can hold onto these until that day of success is mine to live.

Trust

Meditating on Truth

Keep me from deceitful ways; be gracious to me through your law. I have chosen the way of truth; I have set my heart on your laws.

PSALM 119:29-30

When I think about how much time I have spent in my life meditating on half-truths and falsehoods instead of on Your way, it makes me tired. I used all my energy trying to second-guess every good thing in my life. I got used to not trusting any situation or person…or even You. I pray for Your protection, Lord. Keep me in the truth of Your laws. I want to trust Your way without hesitation.

As I walk in Your truth and seek it with longing and intention, I will only meditate on that which is from You and of You. Keep me from the edge of doubt so that I do not follow the path of false teachings and waste more precious time.

Been There

Though you have made me see troubles, many and bitter, you will restore my life again; from the depths of the earth you will again bring me up. You will increase my honor and comfort me once again.

PSALM 71:20-21

The beauty of having been there in the hard times is that I have been there during the good times and the moments of redemption that follow. Lord, I trust You with my life, and I am beginning to release other people to Your care as well. By following Your way and trusting You to restore me to a new creation, I can bring honor to You.

There is great comfort in knowing I have a place to turn. I do not know how other people grow to trust the way life unfolds. I place my hope in that which is sure and true. I give my heart, my life to You.

Through Seeing

But we ought always to thank God for you, brothers loved by the Lord, because from the beginning God chose you to be saved through the sanctifying work of the Spirit and through belief in the truth.

2 THESSALONIANS 2:13

God, thank You for the people in my life who offer me safe places and safe relationships that show me how to trust. Their adherence to what is true and noble and honorable inspires me to live a godly life. When I watch the Holy Spirit leading the decisions and acts of other people, I do see how Your power works through each person and circumstance.

Lord, help me trust You and Your Spirit just as the faithful followers do. Fill me with the same courage and willingness to be obedient to Your calling and Your will. I have entrusted my eternity to You. May I also learn to entrust my present moment, my now, to You as well.

Entrusting It All

*To you, O LORD, I lift up my soul; in you I trust, O
my God.*

PSALM 25:1-2

Lord, You see how I struggle with sharing parts of
myself with other people. I hold onto bits and pieces of
my life to preserve it. I am reluctant to learn that in
order to create a bond of trust, I need to give to people.
But in my spiritual life I desperately want to learn how
to give myself over to You. My soul longs to be in Your
possession.

Lord, please see beyond my stubborn ways of self-
protection to the heart that does beat for You. Today I
will give You more of myself than ever before. I will
trust You with my decisions, my relationships, my con-
cerns, and my future.

Inspiration

Seeing the Glorious

I pray also that the eyes of your heart may be enlightened in order that you may know the hope to which he has called you, the riches of his glorious inheritance in the saints, and his incomparably great power for us who believe.

EPHESIANS 1:18-19

The view of the world through my eyes is obstructed by my many wants and needs. They build up and create barriers which are too high to climb and certainly too big to see around. Clear away this messiness and give my heart eyes that see the outline of hope up ahead. May a rainbow of Your promises—Your kept promises and those to follow—shine brightly on the horizon.

I keep walking toward this beautiful image, and I feel the power of my faith enable me to walk past troubles and obstacles as I make my way toward what I know to be Your glory.

Inspire Me

We continually remember before our God and Father your work produced by faith, your labor prompted by love, and your endurance inspired by hope in our Lord Jesus Christ.

1 THESSALONIANS 1:3

I pray for inspiration and encouragement to come my way. By staying distant from people and commitment, I have chosen to avoid the connections that could inspire me in my faith. This journey is one that requires the help of other people. Why do I resist that so?

God, please make me aware of those people who act out of love, concern, and sincere hope in You. Let their actions be examples that allow me a visible path toward a deeper relationship with You. May I, in turn, take notice of the times when I, too, can be a source of inspiration to another.

Shying Away from Greatness

*Because your sins are so many and your hostility so
great, the prophet is considered a fool, the inspired
man a maniac.*

HOSEA 9:7

I want to express myself, Lord. I want to be free of
all inhibitions, negative self-talk, and the fear of how
other people view me. How many times have I
squelched something that is of You because I did not
want to be viewed as a maniac, a fool? I believe You
speak to us in a language that sometimes is wild and
out-of-the-box. After all, You created the world beyond
the box that we have created for ourselves.

Let me fly high with a sense of song and creation.
Give me the courage to be inspired. Encourage in me
the blossoming of more ideas, more adventures, and
more life.

Mercy

*Have mercy on me, O God, according to your
unfailing love; according to your great compassion
blot out my transgressions. Wash away all my iniq-
uity and cleanse me from my sin.*

PSALM 51:1-2

Oh, have mercy on me, Lord! Let Your unfailing
love and great compassion rain down on my spirit.
Order all that is not of You to fall away from my life. Call
out the sin and rid my heart from all that is dark. Let the
sea of Your grace wash over my iniquities. Only Your
mercy brings peace to my spirit and grace to my life.

Peace

The Peace of Your Countenance

Restore us, O God Almighty; make your face shine upon us, that we may be saved.

PSALM 80:7

When I first looked at You, Lord, Your face radiated Your mercy, and my life was illuminated with peace. I was coming from a time of working against myself, You, and life. I seemed to view everything as a "me against them" situation. Your peace changed that. You restored my balance and my understanding of people.

Now when I turn to face other people, I offer them peace. I speak words of kindness. I extend forgiveness readily. I do not hold back my affection or joy in who they are. I accept them as You accept me. And I am saved.

Keep Me

The LORD bless you and keep you; the LORD make his face shine upon you and be gracious to you; the LORD turn his face toward you and give you peace.

NUMBERS 6:24-26

Chaos can turn my world upside down. But the real danger is if I let it turn my spiritual world upside down. When my gaze is not turned to You, chaos causes me to question You and how You work. I watch reports of disasters or observe a person making decisions that hurt other people, and I cannot take my eyes off the bad news.

But when I turn back to see You and Your glory, my eyes are opened to the peace offerings that exist everywhere. Time after time You give us opportunities to feel the safety of being kept in Your arms and Your presence. But You do not force us to stay here. You allow the chaos of our decisions to play out. I pray for the strength and understanding to choose Your peace all the days of my life.

Peace of the Lord

*Now may the Lord of peace himself give you peace
at all times and in every way.*

2 THESSALONIANS 3:16

Lord, help me to understand Your peace in a way that serves Your will. I tend to seek it when it serves my situation. "Let a friend get over that thing I said," "May my boss be passive today," etc. Other times I beat myself up because I do not seem to have an ounce of peace in me to deal with a moment of turmoil or a testing of my patience.

God, may You grant me the peace of Your mercy and grace at all times. May I not decide which situation warrants peace, but take it on as my spiritual philosophy for all situations. God, help me see that Your peace is part of the grace I received when I met You. It is not something You only parcel out once in a while. I limit what I can do for Your glory until I live the way of peace.

Where I End

*Do not withhold your mercy from me, O LORD; may
your love and your truth always protect me.*

PSALM 40:11

Lord, where my human strength ends, Your eternal
might begins. Where my limited view of love and compassion stops seeing the needs around me, Your love
and compassion continues, reveals, and covers the
needs that arise. I feel so safe knowing that I do not have
to be God in this relationship. There are earthly relationships where I try to play this grand role and fail mis-
erably. But You do not ask me to be mighty and
all-powerful. You ask me to run to Your mercy and Your
truth because once I am there, I am saved from the
falseness of self-reliance.

Take me into the fold of Your love and give me the
peace of complete surrender.

Grace

Return to You

*And the God of all grace, who called you to his
eternal glory in Christ, after you have suffered a
little while, will himself restore you and make you
strong, firm and steadfast. To him be the power for
ever and ever. Amen.*

1 PETER 5:10-11

I am gathering my wounds, my weaknesses, and my
worries and bringing them to You, Lord. I thought I
should warn You because it is quite a load. The experiences I have had with suffering created baggage…
things that seem to cause me to stumble even now. I
thought dragging around evidence of my past mistakes
was a sign of strength. They are a heavy burden, and
now I realize that I will never be strong until I release
them to Your grace.

Receive this junk, this stuff of my life. Restore me
with Your strength and mercy. Now that I will not be
spending my time moving emotional baggage from here
to there and back again, I will be able to serve You
better, Lord. It is good to return to You.

Teach Me

Grace and peace be yours in abundance through the knowledge of God and of Jesus our Lord.

2 PETER 1:2

Often I feel in the dark. There was a time I thought I knew it all, and the world made sense. Yet if one thing countered that view, I was a mess for days. Now I am smart enough to know that I only know a little bit about how the world and other people work, which leaves me back in the dark, Lord.

Lead me to the sources of knowledge, Lord. Give me the discipline and desire to take in all that You want me to learn about You. Great conversations, insightful books, Scripture, and the skill of observation—let these be a part of my daily life so that I can immerse my mind in Your knowledge and my spirit in Your wisdom.

Getting Ready

Therefore, prepare your minds for action; be self-controlled; set your hope fully on the grace to be given you when Jesus Christ is revealed.

1 PETER 1:13

In the days of my childhood, time had little meaning unless it was relevant to a need. When can I eat? When can I sleep? But now I see that time does not exist to fill my needs. It runs beneath our spirits with undetectable speed as we go about our day. It carries us closer to eternity with such a quiet force that when we do finally notice where we are in the continuum of time, we are amazed and shocked. How could it be a year later...a new season...a different stage of life?

God, help me be truly awake these days so that I take in all that Your grace provides. You did not sacrifice for me so that I would waste my days. Prepare me to be self-disciplined, to have hope, and to be ready to receive every ounce of grace from You.

By Grace

For it is by grace you have been saved, through faith—and this not from yourselves, it is the gift of God—not by works, so that no one can boast. For we are God's workmanship, created in Christ Jesus to do good works, which God prepared in advance for us to do.

EPHESIANS 2:8-10

Those who knew me before my step into faith might think I have been saved by the skin of my teeth. I just consider it a miracle. God, I know that there is not anything I have done to deserve the grace You have bestowed upon my life. My transformation is not merely a change of habits, attitudes, and philosophies. It is an inside-out change that can only be explained as the work of Your hand.

When people ask how I have been able to produce good works, I will not search for a list of things I have done to create such success. I need only point to You, my Creator and the Giver of all grace.

Help

Spare Me

O LORD my God, I called to you for help and you healed me. O LORD, you brought me up from the grave; you spared me from going down into the pit.

PSALM 30:2-3

As a flippant teenager I used to say, "Spare me" whenever I wanted to skip to something better. "Spare me the details" or "Spare me the boring lecture." It is funny how the meaning of those words changed after I experienced hardship. Spare me…it is no longer my sarcastic way to end a conversation. It is my frequent plea to You.

Lord, pull me from my despair and the depths of my self-pity. Place me on new heights so that I can stand tall and gain perspective once again of the life You have given to me. Spare me from the fate of my own demise. Help me.

First Things

O LORD, save us; O LORD, grant us success.

PSALM 118:25

God, is my desire for success pleasing to You? Am I keeping in line with Your will? I must say, it is hard to know sometimes. I start each day with good intentions, but I know that my own desires begin to dictate my decisions and the path of my success. I know that all good things are born of Your heart. I know that my ability comes from You. Help me first understand that it is Your saving grace that allows me to move forward at all.

Give me insight to see how to turn, how to lead, how to be. Grant me success as it pleases You, and not as it suits my five-year plan, Lord. I pray for Your help because I no longer want to act as though this journey is one I make alone.

Come and Get Me

I have strayed like a lost sheep. Seek your servant,
for I have not forgotten your commands.

PSALM 119:176

As a human, I love to be found. To be found is to belong to another person or to a group or to a community. To be found is to be loved and known. God, I have strayed to a place that is far from Your hand and Your way. And I know that only through Your grace do I have the ability to ask this one more time: Please come and get me. Find me, Lord. Help me return to the place of Your presence.

Your commands are written upon my heart. Though I have strayed, I have never lost my faith in Your Word and Your love. Seek me out, Lord. Find me. It is to You that I want to belong forever.

My Backbone

May integrity and uprightness protect me, because my hope is in you.

PSALM 25:21

In my faith, I have discovered the secret to standing tall in the world. When I threw away my desire to put myself first, I came upon Your will and Your purpose for my life. This gift has given me the security to be at peace with the way life unfolds. My hope is not in guaranteed profit, certain success, or the perfect relationship. My hope is in You, and when I face choices and changes, I measure my response according to the integrity Your love gives to me.

To be secure in a loving and knowing God, I knew I would have to let go of my unreal expectations so that I could make room for Your unbelievable promises. It was the best decision I ever made. Thank You for giving me what I needed to stand tall and to walk with hope.

Protection

*Then Jacob prayed, "O God of my father Abraham,
God of my father Isaac, O LORD, who said to me,
'Go back to your country and your relatives, and I
will make you prosper,' I am unworthy of all the
kindness and faithfulness you have shown your servant. I had only my staff when I crossed this Jordan,
but now I have become two groups. Save me, I pray,
from the hand of my brother Esau, for I am afraid
he will come and attack me, and also the mothers
with their children. But you have said, 'I will surely
make you prosper and will make your descendants
like the sand of the sea, which cannot be counted.'"*

GENESIS 32:9-12

God, You provide a secure way for me to head into
today and the future days of my life. When I stumble,
You offer Your hand and lead me through the situation.
I have learned faith through the act of perseverance.
And I have discovered hope on the other side. Lead me,
Lord. Guard my heart from becoming hardened or
untrusting. I turn my fragile spirit over to Your care, for
You are my Father, my Maker, and my Protector.

Perseverance

Holding On

In your hands are strength and power to exalt and give strength to all. Now, our God, we give you thanks, and praise your glorious name.

1 CHRONICLES 29:12-13

Lord, help me see through the present struggles and into the future peace You have for me. Give me the calm of this peace now, as I try to regain perspective—Your perspective—to see this through. I pray that You will keep holding onto me as I try to hold onto my sense of thanksgiving and praise. Turn my thoughts from selfish regrets to generous ideas and hopes.

Your strength is my strength. When will I truly believe this and rest in Your power? The ground I stand on is shaky, but the hand I hold onto is not. For that I thank You, Lord.

Faithfully Yours

Your word, O LORD, is eternal; it stands firm in the heavens. Your faithfulness continues through all generations; you established the earth, and it endures. Your laws endure to this day, for all things serve you.

PSALM 119:89-91

I do not often speak in terms of faithfulness. God, open my eyes to Your faithfulness. There is evidence of it all around me. May I, in turn, infuse my daily existence with this gift by following through, considering other people, and serving in this life You have given me.

Before I doubt another person or situation, let me first look at my own level of commitment. Am I faithful to this friend, this project, this effort? Show me what I can do to display commitment and to honor You with a life that is faithfully Yours.

Lessons to Take Along

*Teach me to do your will, for you are my God; may
your good Spirit lead me on level ground.*

PSALM 143:10

I look at old photos and think about how I look,
what I was doing, who my friends were, and what life
was like. Maybe what I should examine are the lessons
You were teaching me at that stage of my life. I pray to
be taught Your will through the wisdom of other people
and the experiences that come my way. I believe that I
can learn a lot right now that will help me later on as I
keep walking toward higher and more level ground.

It takes perseverance to go from the lowlands to the
top of the mountain. I pray that as I piece together the
times of my life from memory and wisdom, I will have
a greater understanding of how perseverance is not only
possible, but is a natural part of the faith journey.

Striving for Strong Faith

For this very reason, make every effort to add to your faith goodness; and to goodness, knowledge; and to knowledge, self-control; and to self-control, perseverance; and to perseverance, godliness; and to godliness, brotherly kindness; and to brotherly kindness, love.

2 PETER 1:5-7

I like to add onto my on-line shopping cart. When standing in line at the store, I am the first to add a point-of-purchase item to my basket. Anytime I play a game, I always want to be the one to gain an extra point for the win. But Lord, I realize how little I have added to my faith lately. I discover in Your Word so many qualities You hope I will desire. You reveal what a person with a godly heart desires and represents.

Hear my prayer, Lord. I want my eyes to be opened to opportunities for spiritual growth. I pray to add to my faith so that I multiply the spiritual fruit of my life's harvest.

Discernment

All Is Fair

Then you will understand what is right and just and fair—every good path. For wisdom will enter your heart, and knowledge will be pleasant to your soul. Discretion will protect you, and understanding will guard you.

PROVERBS 2:9-11

Live and let live. To each his own. All Is fair in love and war. Lord, these actually were philosophies I was clinging to as I made my way from yesterday to today. I created all kinds of theories that gave me breathing room and allowed me to not take responsibility for the fairness or unfairness of the situations in which I played a role.

Fill me with the wisdom that sees past my own nose and interests. Move me through circumstances so that I can feel the joy of knowledge that embraces justice and compassion. May I guard my heart with discretion and discernment so the philosophies of old do not shape my understanding and my perspective again.

Go Right Ahead

*I will praise the L*ORD*, who counsels me; even at night my heart instructs me. I have set the L*ORD *always before me. Because he is at my right hand, I will not be shaken.*

PSALM 16:7-8

Lord, go before me and create a path for me to follow. I give my days ahead to You and Your service. Instruct me as I eat, sleep, and pray so that I am not filled with questions that can lead me astray in a weak moment. You are the Model of the heart I long for. You are my Counselor and Redeemer who knows the way through the mountains and canyons.

I take each step with my eyes on Your might. Let my commitment of faith be transformed into wisdom and love. And may I never be so sure of my pace that I desire to pass You and take over the lead on this journey.

Shed the Light

*Who can discern his errors? Forgive my hidden
faults....May the words of my mouth and the meditation of my heart be pleasing in your sight, O
LORD, my Rock and my Redeemer.*

PSALM 19:12,14

Nobody really wants to know their faults, especially
if it means that other people can see them, too. But I am
beginning to understand why it is so important to
understand my problems, my flaws, my weaknesses.
God, You are my safe place. I pray for You to gently
reveal those areas in which I can be stronger, kinder,
more aware.

I desire to live a life that is pleasing to You. I know
this does not happen overnight. Give me the blessings
of insight and discernment. Only when I accept these
blessings can I truly embrace who I am in You.

Knowledge

All of the Above

Do you know how God controls the clouds and makes his lightning flash? Do you know how the clouds hang poised, those wonders of him who is perfect in knowledge?

JOB 37:15-16

When other people ask about You, I am at a loss for words and answers. Like taking quizzes in high school when I was always tempted to answer "all of the above" or "none of the above," I look for a blanket statement that saves my face and faith. I pray to be a more faithful reader and prayer of Your Word so that I do not miss the opportunities before me to deepen my faith and that of other people.

For now my "all of the above" answer to faith-and-life questions is "it's all from above." The answers are all with You and from You and of You. That knowledge is really all any of us need to hold onto.

Direct My Steps

Then Saul prayed to the LORD, the God of Israel,
"Give me the right answer."

1 SAMUEL 14:41

Lord, is this one of those times when any choice is okay with You, as long as I stay in Your ways and wisdom? Or is this really a fork in the road that has a blatant "of God" and "not of God" option? Forgive me for not having this understanding. I am still learning to communicate with You and learning to hear the discerning voice of Your Spirit.

Please direct my feet, my mouth, my heart so that I follow in the way that is right for me and for Your will. I pray as Saul did. Give me the right answer, Lord.

Your Ingredients

*Your hands made me and formed me; give me
understanding to learn your commands.*

PSALM 119:73

I thank You today and every day for shaping me,
forming my very spirit and soul, Lord. I have come to
know You so personally because my heart has desired
to return to its Maker. This longing leads me back to
You over and over, even when I wander and follow a
path of my own creation.

I am made with Your ingredients. My strengths and
weaknesses all blend together beneath Your hand so
that I become this complex self. I know whose hand
created me. Now I pray for the knowledge to understand and follow Your commands. This complex being
You made as "me" has been created just for this life, for
these very personal circumstances and choices. May I
follow Your commands so that Your creation is used for
the purposes You intended.

Willing Student

Teach me knowledge and good judgment, for I believe in your commands. Before I was afflicted I went astray, but now I obey your word.

PSALM 119:66-67

I want to be taught by the Master. Remind me each day how precious time is and how much I still have to learn about faith and life from my Creator. My willingness to invest in my spiritual education must begin now. I believe in Your Word and Your wisdom. Please help me pay attention to Your commands. When I want to glide through days on end without learning, bring my heart to attention.

Lord, I will need help following through with this discipline, but I am eager to study and obey Your Word. Share Your knowledge with this willing student.

Healing

Be merciful to me, LORD, for I am faint; O LORD,
heal me, for my bones are in agony. My soul is in
anguish. How long, O LORD, how long?

PSALM 6:2-3

It is easy to break as a human. As a being made of earth, water, and breath, it is easy to crumble and develop holes. Lord, You made me. You know what it takes to heal the places that are broken, underused, and weak.

I give to You my physical, emotional, and spiritual wounds and ask for Your touch, Your breath, Your mercy to cover them. Heal me, Lord.

Physical

No Charge

As you go, preach this message: "The kingdom of heaven is near." Heal the sick, raise the dead, cleanse those who have leprosy, drive out demons. Freely you have received, freely give. Do not take along any gold or silver or copper in your belts; take no bag for the journey, or extra tunic, or sandals or a staff; for the worker is worth his keep.

MATTHEW 10:7-10

Doctors, appointments, and expensive medications...that is what I consider it takes for physical healing. That is what our place in time and society offers us. But Lord, I look back on the way You healed those in need of physical help. It was done out of Your power and without cost, without strings, without obligation. You even sent out Your disciples with instruction to not take anything in exchange for healing other people.

Lord, when I face the need for physical healing, may my heart first come to You in prayer and with requests for healing. I will pray for my doctors and for my ability to make wise health decisions. And after I pay my deductible to humans, I will thank You for the "free of charge" healing of the spirit that takes place each time I pray.

After the Healing

When Jesus came into Peter's house, he saw Peter's mother-in-law lying in bed with a fever. He touched her hand and the fever left her, and she got up and began to wait on him.

MATTHEW 8:14-15

You hear my prayers for healing and wholeness, Lord. I call out to You during a night of pain and heartache. I believe in Your healing touch. When Your peace replaces my brokenness, I pray that I will be grateful. When my fatigue eases into energy and strength, I pray that I will in turn wait on You and obey Your commands with renewed commitment.

Lord, You touched me and healed me. I praise You, and may I never forget who is the Light when I come out of the darkness.

Cover Me

Keep me, O LORD, from the hands of the wicked; protect me from men of violence who plan to trip my feet.

PSALM 140:4

Lord, save me from my fear of the unknown. I read and see enough news about the violence that exists beyond my front door. Do not let this consume me, this possible pain. Give me courage to trust You with the steps I take beyond this threshold. Lord, I believe You will protect me. And if something should happen, I believe You would not abandon me.

I know I cannot avoid living fully just because there is risk of physical harm. Keep me from harm's way. Speak to my heart and give me the presence of mind to listen to Your guidance.

Remembering to Ask

Jesus stopped and ordered the man to be brought to him. When he came near, Jesus asked him, "What do you want me to do for you?" "Lord, I want to see," he replied. Jesus said to him, "Receive your sight; your faith has healed you." Immediately he received his sight and followed Jesus, praising God. When all the people saw it, they also praised God.

LUKE 18:40-43

I believe I have carried around this hurt for a long time. I might find temporary solutions that ease the discomfort or ways to distract my mind from the pain, but I have not done the most basic thing. I have not told You, my God and Savior, what I need. I have not prayed for healing.

God, my own uncertainties have kept me from falling at Your feet and asking You for help. Give me the strength to hold onto this kind of faith at all times. I pray that my circumstance will become an opportunity for other people to see Your power and to praise Your mighty name.

Emotional

Save My Heart

Turn to me and be gracious to me, for I am lonely and afflicted. The troubles of my heart have multiplied; free me from my anguish.

PSALM 25:16-17

Look at me, God. I am sad…lonely even. It takes so much for my heart to feel alive these days. I am so distant from those things that used to bring me joy. Look at me, Lord. This is not who I want to be. This is not who You want Your child to be.

Turn to me, Lord. Heal my brokenness so that I can hold my faith in the warmth of the sun and carry it with me throughout the day. I do not know when I changed so drastically. But I do know that You have not changed. You are the Healer of wounds inside and out. You are the One who sees me and sees my trouble without turning away. Turn to me. Let me feel the sun. Turn to me.

Stepping Out of the Fog

Do not conform any longer to the pattern of this world, but be transformed by the renewing of your mind. Then you will be able to test and approve what God's will is—his good, pleasing and perfect will.

ROMANS 12:2

My mind is foggy. I have stepped behind a shroud of stress, distance, and emotional indifference. I view everything through this haze. My mind makes decisions while surrounded by the cloud of nothingness. I want to walk through my life awake and with great passion, Lord. Pull me away from the self-protective layer.

Renew my mind and my heart, Lord. While I thought I was getting by in life, surviving, You have wanted me to be living within Your will. You desire for me to feel the emotional highs and lows which create the landscape of life. I am ready to wake up, Lord.

The Fear Factor

Then Peter got down out of the boat, walked on the water and came toward Jesus. But when he saw the wind, he was afraid and, beginning to sink, cried out, "Lord, save me!"

MATTHEW 14:29-30

Give me courage, Lord. Facing risk is not just a matter of trusting You. It also becomes a matter of defying the power of fear. When Peter walked on the water at Your command, he was held up, kept from being hurt by the storm's strength. But as soon as he let the fear and doubt creep back into his spirit, he began to sink.

I do not want to go under the waves of worry that are just waiting to crash down upon me. Lord, carry me to the shore of emotional safety. Protect my mind from anxiousness. I will keep my eyes upon You, and I will believe You can do the impossible.

Spiritual

Saving Grace

Then they cried to the LORD in their trouble, and he saved them from their distress. He sent forth his word and healed them; he rescued them from the grave.

PSALM 107:19-20

Lord, I was proud, and You humbled me. I was selfish, and You showed me compassion. I was cold, and You taught me to feel. I was empty, and You filled me. I was dark, and You brought me into the light.

The power of Your Word came into my being, and I have been saved. Once I looked at my life as meaningless and without purpose beyond physical and material pursuits. Now I understand that my life is one to be lived spiritually and within Your grace. I was unloved, and now I am loved.

Laundry Day

*I said, "O LORD, have mercy on me; heal me, for I
have sinned against you."*

PSALM 41:4

Don't we all have dirty laundry that we hang out for
other people to see? Some days I walk around littering
every place I go with my spiritual dirty laundry. Is it that
I do not care what people think? Or that I do not care
about my spirit enough to carry my sin to You as You
call me to do?

Lord, receive me and my dirty laundry today. I
know it is quite a pile. I was chatting away about grace
to everyone instead of actually coming to You to receive
that grace. I was talking up salvation to my unsaved
neighbors, while privately ignoring the urge to praise
You and ask for forgiveness. And as they say, all these
dirty items in my life are starting to smell to high
heaven. It is definitely time for a laundry day.

Whole Again

Create in me a pure heart, O God, and renew a steadfast spirit within me. Do not cast me from your presence or take your Holy Spirit from me. Restore to me the joy of your salvation and grant me a willing spirit, to sustain me.

PSALM 51:10-12

My joy is complete in You, Lord. The holes in my spirit created by doubt or pain are filled, and I am renewed as a believer, as a child of God. My spirit knows the hand of its Healer, and it soars in Your presence. As I pray to You, my life is resurrected and my spirit is willing and able to keep following You and Your ways.

Your grace cleanses me from my past mistakes, my times of weakness or trouble, and You have made me new again. When I am reluctant to recognize this because I want to do things my way or take credit for my state of grace, my spirit reminds me that You are the faithful healer of all things past, present, and future. I am merely the vessel in need of Your healing. I pray to really see myself whole and renewed, and I acknowledge Your salvation and mercy.

Worship

Blessed be your glorious name, and may it be exalted above all blessing and praise. You alone are the LORD. You made the heavens, even the highest heavens, and all their starry host, the earth and all that is on it, the seas and all that is in them. You give life to everything, and the multitudes of heaven worship you.

NEHEMIAH 9:5-6

Praise. Reverence. Vulnerability. When I take time to worship You and thank You for all that You are, I feel the longing to praise rise up in my spirit. I become humble and aware of my weakness. I realize how much I need to come to You just to get through each day. I question why I would ever resist this pull toward Your Spirit.

May I learn to worship You with the awe and wonder my Creator deserves. And may I leave a time of such prayer and praise with a deeper sense of how much I love the One who first loved me.

Praise

You Alone

And Hezekiah prayed to the LORD: "O LORD, God of Israel, enthroned between the cherubim, you alone are God over all the kingdoms of the earth. You have made heaven and earth."

2 KINGS 19:15

You alone formed my mind and body. You alone formed the land on which I walk and sculpted the curve of the earth. You alone know my past, present, and future. Lord and Creator, You are so worthy of praise. May my words and deeds express my love and praise to You each day.

I rule over a few scattered decisions. You are Ruler over the course of all life. I pray that I am worthy to be called Yours and that my motives are always to glorify You alone—my God, my Creator, my Lord.

Almighty

The heavens praise your wonders, O LORD, your faithfulness too, in the assembly of the holy ones. For who in the skies above can compare with the LORD?...O LORD God Almighty, who is like you? You are mighty, O LORD, and your faithfulness surrounds you.

PSALM 89:5-6,8

The world considers mightiness to be measured in muscles and influence. But Lord, You are almighty, and Your strength surpasses my human understanding of power. Since the beginning of time, Your creation has bowed down before You. Who or what else can possibly compare with Your grace and Your authority?

Lord, You rule over all creation, and still Your faithfulness is evident in my humble life. I love You because Your power does not force people from Your presence. The strength of Your love calls people to Your heart.

Let the Word Out

I will extol the LORD at all times; his praise will always be on my lips. My soul will boast in the LORD; let the afflicted hear and rejoice. Glorify the LORD with me; let us exalt his name together.

PSALM 34:1-3

When You listen to my speech after a long day, do You hear words that praise You, that please You? Help me to be more careful of the way I speak or express my emotions. May I be mindful that praises spoken throughout a good day or during the hard times can fall upon the ears and hearts of those who desperately want to believe in You.

By glorifying Your name, I am telling other people that I am Yours. I show them that when I am weak, it is Your strength that pulls me through, and when I am strong, it is Your love that is carrying me each step of the way.

Reverence

Promise-Keeper

O LORD, God of Israel, there is no God like you in heaven above or on earth below—you who keep your covenant of love with your servants who continue wholeheartedly in your way. You have kept your promise to your servant David my father; with your mouth you have promised and with your hand you have fulfilled it—as it is today.

1 KINGS 8:23-24

God, Your promises are sacred. I build a life upon these gifts of hope. My steps have faltered over the years, but I always regain my balance when I make my way back to these promises. You keep a covenant with me even when my focus wanders away from faith. You do not deny me when I come to be in Your presence.

Lord, it is in Your hand that I can be free. It is under Your will that I find my true path. And it is as I praise You and honor You with my life that I discover the beauty of these promises.

Awe

LORD, I have heard of your fame; I stand in awe of
your deeds, O LORD. Renew them in our day, in our
time make them known; in wrath remember mercy.

HABAKKUK 3:2

Before I knew You personally, I had friends who
loved You. Even when I would challenge such belief, I
was always watching for the signs of Your existence.
Lord, through the lens of my friends' faith, I began to
see how You cared for those who put their faith in Your
way. I saw the gift of renewal and the impact of Your
influence in all that they did and said, even when they
were struggling to understand You.

Lord, now I am so thankful to know You. And while
I strive to define my faith and live it out for other people
to see, I pray for Your awesome touch to find me and
my life. Let other people be in awe of the God I know.

Better than Life

I have seen you in the sanctuary and beheld your power and your glory. Because your love is better than life, my lips will glorify you. I will praise you as long as I live, and in your name I will lift up my hands. My soul will be satisfied as with the richest of foods; with singing lips my mouth will praise you.

PSALM 63:2-5

I found myself obsessing over the monthly bills the other day. I went over the numbers again and again, willing them to be different. It was not until later that afternoon that I paid attention to all that was going on outside my window. You had given me a beautiful day—spectacular and glorious. I was just a few feet away from Your sanctuary and a day of saying praises, yet I had wasted time on something as temporal as bills.

Lord, I pray for soul satisfaction that does not depend on physical comforts. Let the greatness of my God satisfy me like an endless banquet of food and provision. May I begin each tomorrow by first approaching Your heart and offering up my gratitude.

Vulnerability

See It All

Search me, O God, and know my heart; test me and know my anxious thoughts. See if there is any offensive way in me, and lead me in the way everlasting.

PSALM 139:23-24

Well, I might as well face it: By now You know me and my faults. You have seen me yell at my spouse, neglect someone who needed attention, take the easy way out to avoid commitment, etc. And these are just the faults I am willing to speak of today. The fact that You know me so well and still love me is one of life's greatest mysteries. I realize that I still try to keep my transgressions from You sometimes. I even try to keep them from myself.

But here I am, asking for You to see it all—the good, the bad—and show me what is next for me. Now that You know me, I pray to become the person You know I can be.

Correct Me

Yet you know me, O LORD; you see me and test my thoughts about you.

JEREMIAH 12:3

Correct me if I am wrong about You, Lord. I believe that I have led a life that has been a bit off-kilter because I do not know You as well as I should. I long to have the kind of connection that puts me at ease in Your presence and replaces my doubts and questions with certainty. Search my ways of thinking, my pattern of emotions, and my view of the world, and repair any false perspectives I have.

God, I pray for knowledge that gives me a greater understanding of You. See me and test my thoughts about You to see if they are strong in truth. I want to know You. I pray to be open to Your correction and testing. I pray to give myself over to You fully.

Hold That Thought

You discern my going out and my lying down; you are familiar with all my ways. Before a word is on my tongue you know it completely, O LORD.

PSALM 139:3-4

Thank goodness I caught some regrettable words before they left my mouth and entered the mind of another person. However, You heard what thoughts I was forming. You heard the attitude and my unwillingness to extend kindness. This is the kind of relationship we have: I seek You, and You already know me inside and out.

I pray that as my faith grows stronger and deeper, I will not have to hold back so many thoughts and words. I pray for a purer view of life and people. Give me a compassionate heart so I reach out with words of comfort and peace, rather than stinging lines of controversy or division. May my familiar ways be pleasing to You, Lord.

Thanksgiving

Then Hannah prayed and said: "My heart rejoices in the Lord; in the Lord my horn is lifted high. My mouth boasts over my enemies, for I delight in your deliverance. There is no one holy like the Lord; there is no one besides you; there is no Rock like our God."

1 SAMUEL 2:1-2

I rejoice in You, my Lord. I find salvation in Your love and grace. Only when I depend on You for everything am I free to experience Your abundance. I pray that when trouble or want finds me, I will not turn from You or deny my faith. As I stand on the mountaintop of joy, may I remember the view and return to this spot at all times. My praises shall fill the canyon below and the sky above.

I hope to make gratitude my offering to You each day. Through my speech, my actions, and my efforts, may You know that I am so very thankful for You.

Dependence

The Song I Sing

*I will praise God's name in song and glorify him
with thanksgiving.*

PSALM 69:30

When I reach a goal, the glory is Yours, Lord. When
I experience a time of plenty, may words of thanksgiving pour from my lips. If I fall, stumbling because of
my own blindness, I will express my thanksgiving
before You help me back up. My faith is my song. My
heart knows the lyrics, and my spirit whistles the tune
when I need comfort.

When I look at how far I have come in my faith, I
am so very grateful to belong to You, my Redeemer.

Your Strength

*Help us, O LORD our God, for we rely on you, and
in your name we have come against this vast army.
O LORD, you are our God; do not let man prevail
against you.*

2 CHRONICLES 14:11

There are times when I feel there is an army just outside my front door waiting to take me down. The fear builds up because I am focused on my strength and not on Yours. God, help me to rely on You and turn to You even when I feel the fear building.

Do not let me fall back on my own ability when I have the source of Your might to pull me through. I am so thankful that You do not ask me to go it alone. When I look to You for direction and encouragement, I have already won the battle.

What You Give

For I gave them the words you gave me and they accepted them. They knew with certainty that I came from you, and they believed that you sent me. I pray for them. I am not praying for the world, but for those you have given me, for they are yours.

JOHN 17:8-9

When I cannot think of anything to say, please give me the words that are needed. There are people in my life who need advice, counsel, wisdom, and help. When I search my mind for the perfect thing to say, I draw a blank. I can only turn them toward You. May they see my dependence upon You so that they will have confidence in the words You give me to share.

These people are the ones I pray for most. You know them and their personal journeys, and I am thankful that You entrust them to me…people for me to know, to pray for, and to care about.

Leaning on Your Wisdom

*God gave Solomon wisdom and very great insight,
and a breadth of understanding as measureless as
the sand on the seashore.*

1 KINGS 4:29

My hope for wisdom is grounded in my faith in Your promises. If I am left to my own devices and motivation, I will never understand the world around me. And it is not only these external mysteries I long to explore. I hope to discover more about my own heart and mind and my Creator.

I depend upon Your wisdom, Lord. Free my mind of the half-truths, untruths, and misconceptions so my growth is not hindered by lies and foolishness. I pray that the way I use my gift of wisdom will reflect my thankful heart.

Abundance

From Your Hand

*O LORD our God, as for all this abundance that we
have provided for building you a temple for your
Holy Name, it comes from your hand, and all of it
belongs to you.*

1 CHRONICLES 29:16

I look around me at the blessings I have. Even
though there is much I do not have, I know I live with
abundance. The home I create and offer up to You
through hospitality comes from Your hand. The job I do
so that I can honor You is only possible because of the
talents and strengths You provide.

When I take a step forward, it is because You have
given me the strength and the direction and the motivation. You inspire all that I do. May my spirit of
thanksgiving honor You and return a bit of what You
have given to me.

Surrounded by Your Plenty

They feast on the abundance of your house; you give them drink from your river of delights. For with you is the fountain of life; in your light we see light.

PSALM 36:8-9

You have called me to sit at a table of plenty, Lord. This feast You present is a life of possibilities and love and growth. The banquet is never-ending, and I stay in Your beautiful home not as a guest, but as a family member, a child of Your own. Here the cup is filled with Your life-giving sacrifice and the plate overflows with food for the spirit and soul.

I may face difficulties in this lifetime, and I may even question why I am allowed to sit at this table of abundance, but I know that this gathering of delights is just a glimpse of eternity's joy.

Replenish My Spirit

You gave abundant showers, O God; you refreshed your weary inheritance. Your people settled in it, and from your bounty, O God, you provided for the poor.

PSALM 68:9-10

May Your love rain down on me and refresh my spirit. I open my heart as an empty vessel waiting to be filled by Your abundant grace. For a time I hid from such expressions of Your love. I ran for shelter that did not protect me, but prevented me from encountering Your grace. Even then I knew how powerful it would be to share in Your bountiful mercy.

Lord, thank You for hearing my prayers over the years, and especially in recent days. I have felt a shift in my heart. I know I am closer to You. It is with deep gratitude that I look ahead and realize that Your spiritual abundance will shower down on me when I call upon Your mighty, merciful name.